I0007355

HowExpert Presents

How To Use a 3D Printer

HowExpert with Zachary Hestand

Copyright HowExpert™
www.HowExpert.com

For more tips related to this topic, visit HowExpert.com/3dprinter.

Recommended Resources

- HowExpert.com – Quick 'How To' Guides on All Topics from A to Z by Everyday Experts.
- HowExpert.com/free – Free HowExpert Email Newsletter.
- HowExpert.com/books – HowExpert Books
- HowExpert.com/courses – HowExpert Courses
- HowExpert.com/clothing – HowExpert Clothing
- HowExpert.com/membership – HowExpert Membership Site
- HowExpert.com/affiliates – HowExpert Affiliate Program
- HowExpert.com/writers – Write About Your #1 Passion/Knowledge/Expertise & Become a HowExpert Author.
- HowExpert.com/resources – Additional HowExpert Recommended Resources
- YouTube.com/HowExpert – Subscribe to HowExpert YouTube.
- Instagram.com/HowExpert – Follow HowExpert on Instagram.
- Facebook.com/HowExpert – Follow HowExpert on Facebook.

Table of Contents

Introduction

So you've heard of 3D Printers and you want to find out more about them? Well here's the place to be! I will show you in a 7 step guide what 3d printers are all about, how to use one, and even help you decide which one is right for you!

Chapter 1: Getting Started

1.1 What is a 3D printer?

Well a 3d printer in simplest complex is a printer that makes 3-dimensional objects usually out of plastic. Since we are talking about more consumer based 3D printers, I will stick with the basic type of printer, Fused Deposition modeling (FDM) or Fused filament fabrication (FFF).

What these more complex names mean is basically a machine that will lay down layer after layer of plastic, fusing each layer to the next, ultimately forming the object. To get the picture in your head, think of a hot glue gun how it pushes out that thick goopy glue. Imagine running the hot glue gun in a square, then placing more glue on top of the old glue, and keep doing that until you have a nice little cube.

That is basically what a 3D printer does, at a much more fine level, usually 1/10th to 3/10th of a millimeter. (Sometimes less for super fine detail!) This entire process is automatic however, as the machine will move to do this processes.

1.2 Can I Use a 3d Printer?

This is the true question many ask. Before jumping into the world of 3D printing, think. Do you patience? 3D printing can be a very long process. Do you have the basic skills of tinkering? The more affordable a printer is, the more likely it will malfunction or have flaws. You must be willing to tinker and try to improve on your printer. Do you have the money?

3D printers can be very expensive, from the printer itself, to the filament (plastic) it uses. Finally, one of the most important parts is, what will you use it for? Many people forget to ask themselves this question. A 3D printer is an amazing tool, and can be used in many different applications. If you plan on buying it just for printing the toys, it may get old after a while.

Many use 3D printers for making replicas of things, props, robotics, or any other hobby. Some people even find success in selling their 3d prints; however this goes into an entirely different subject that will be cover later in this guide. Even if you don't have a hobby application for it yet, then maybe it is time for you to get into a hobby that 3d printing can apply to!

Chapter 2: Buying a 3D Printer

So, you have decided to buy a 3d printer! Or you are at least thinking about buying one. I am not going to lie and say this step is easy, it's not. Finding the right printer for your situation, within the right budget is difficult. You will have to do your homework and look at different printer's prices, reviews, specs, and more.

2.1 Price Ranges

3D printers come in different price ranges, just like anything else. I will break them down into 5 different price ranges to make it easier for those that a very specific budget, and the recommend a printer out of the category to check out.

The first range would be the entry level printers. Printers in this price range will be below $500. This is why they are known as entry level, as it's better to try the cheaper alternative then go full blown into something more expensive.

A lot of these printers however, will come as kits rather than a full assembled version. (For the fully assembled version of a lot of kits will put it outside the entry level range) Building a printer can be good for you though, as you learn exactly how it ticks, and will in the future know what to or not to look for when purchasing a better, more sophisticated printer. Printers in this price range are also made with cheaper parts or designs.

Be wary of that and look for printers will good reviews, as you don't want to get a printer that barely works and have to put even more money into it just to get a print.

For the printer I recommend to check out (everyone in fact, it's more than just a budget printer) is the Wanhao I3 V2. This printer has an amazing build, with strong, metal components, a decent 8inx8inx7in build platform, and overall quality parts.

The Wanhao, after fine tuning has been known to outperform printers 2-3 times its price and is also backed by a huge community of people that own one as well. Coming in at $400, this printer is worth checking out!

The next price ranger is dubbed the "affordable" range. Ranging from $500-$750, these printers are usually better built that entry level printers but are still in the *affordable* range for your average consumer.

However, this is also a very strange price range. The printers are very similar to the entry level printers, but paying an extra $250-$500 would put you on the next range and give you significantly a better printer. The one perhaps advantage over the entry level printers is you can find printers in the price range with enclosures, which can help keep noise down, and printer filament that is sensitive to cooling, such as ABS (What Legos are made of).

For this price range it is tough, but one of the most highly rated printers in this range is the Flash forge Finder, at $500. Yes, it sits right at the edge of going into entry level, and you probably could find a used one for less, but even so, it better suits this range with its enclosure, which may be the only thing it has on the Wanhao.

The 3rd range is known as the mid-range printers. Ranging from $750-$1000, these printers are an amazing example of constantly changing technology, and some consider these printers on the lower end of the "high-end" printers, as they perform amazingly, without costing you an arm and a leg. Printers in this price range truly differ from those in the previous ranges, as they have many different options, better builds, bigger build envelopes, and higher quality printing.

This is also the start of the good plug n play machines; they don't require a lot of maintenance, are extremely easy to use, and work out of the box. I would only recommend these printers though for people who either have previous experience in 3d printing, or know they are going to need this no matter what, as this would be an expensive let down if you end up not liking 3d printing.

For the price ranges printer, I would put out the QIDI Tech I. A metal frame, with a decent 8.8in x 5.9in x 5.9in built area. Coming in at about $700 it is at the lower price range of the tier. A further note though on printers in these ranges. With these plug and play designs; you lose customization that earlier ranges were full of. Some printers in these ranges here on up will still be customizable but for many, that is not the case.

The next range is dubbed the enthusiast level. Costs ranging from $1000-$2000, these printers are for none other than the enthusiasts. These printers are some of the best printers on the market, without paying $2000+ dollars. Zortrax M200 is the winner for this price range with some of the best reviews.

Coming in at $1,935, this printer is truly a plug and play machine. Little or no work is needed to be done (except pulling it out of the box) to get it to print quality objects. Now, I am not putting down the M200 saying it is a bad machine or anything, however this is an example of paying more for plug and play. Yes, this machine is made with much more quality parts than (as if you cannot tell by now, I like referencing it) the Wanhao i3, its build platform is only 5mm taller with the exact same X and Y dimensions. Printers in this price range are a lot of times what set people apart from the tinkers to the just users. You don't or can't tinker with most printers in this price range with how they are built.

If something breaks as well, replacement parts can be outrageous, as most parts here are made specifically for each printer and are not something generic. An example of this is the MakerBot 5th generation Smart Extruder. The extruder itself is quite smart in some cases, having the capability to detect jams, if you run out of filament and more.

If this extruder were to break after its 6 month warranty, it will set you back $200. Be warry of things like this, you don't want to have to save for months and month for example, buy it, and have to pay even more money. Read reviews and information in this price range as well.Now finally, we come to the last price range. These printers are known as premium level printers. These printers are the ones that exceed $2000.

When you buy one of these, you are buying something that usually has features none other has, from huge build areas, special duel extruders, and more over all ease of use. Another relevant printer in this price range is the SLA printer, which uses lasers in a resin to cure an object with extreme detail.

However, I will not go any farther into this form of 3d printing, as the upkeep and cleanup is outrageous in price and mess. These really are not consumer printers so to say, and are better for companies for fine detail prototyping or jewelers. The printer I have selected from this price range is based off of what I have seen and heard about it and is none other than the Raise 3D N2. This printer comes with a full enclosure, a led touch screen, a massive 12in x 12in x 12in build area, dual extruder options as well as more.

This printer also has the capability to print resolutions of .01 compared to the fine detail most printers can print at is .1. This printer also has incredible features such as one of my favorites, print saving on power lose. If you lose power to a printer for most every printer, you "lose" the print, as the only way to continue is to either restart the entire print, or measure and print the remaining parts of the print separately. With the Raise 3D N2, this will not happen!

Now think long and hard about your choice. Your choice will ultimately reflect your experience with 3d printers. If you buy a bad printer, you are in for a rough road ahead of fixing. If you buy a tinker's printer, be prepared to tinker with it for obvious reasons to improve on its original design to make it better. And if you cough up the money for a high end printer, you will likely find it extremely easy, unless this "quality" printer turns out to be a not so quality. Read reviews, as you did this guide. Join groups dedicated to 3d printing and ask questions. All I can say now is, good luck finding your printer!

Chapter 3: Setting up

Wow! You got yourself a 3D printer! Congratulations, this is a huge step into the world of 3D printing for obvious reasons. Now if you're just reading along to see what's up ahead, no worries, you can use the portion of the guide to understand what it will take from you to operate a 3d printer. Now I will do my best do be as detailed as possible, but at the same time I must remain generic, as different printers will have different set ups, and things needed to be done before your first print. Use this as a general guidance only. Follow all documentation given to you as closely as possible, as that will be your true guide on what to do.

3.1 Unboxing

Now we get to the box, the only thing that is holding you back from your 3d printer. Now this is part is very essential and I advise for you to read carefully. The first thing you want to do before unboxing is check the box itself for damage. 3d printers typically do not like to be jarred, hit, etc. as this can damage all sorts of different pieces.

Take pictures of any areas of concern, such as dents, rips, or even if the box looks opened and resealed. This is proof you can use later on if your printer is missing pieces or damaged in any sort of way to get a free replacement/parts. Now before you open the box, look for warnings that tell you not to open the box with a knife or something sharp.

Sometimes the printer components could be right underneath the top, so you don't want to accidently cut some. Once you have it open, take out any paperwork that is usually at the top. Read through it and see if it has any unboxing instructions. If not, continue to pull your printer out carefully in a nice open area. If something doesn't want to come out, check to make sure it doesn't have another piece attached to it.

Now take any Styrofoam out of the way once the printer has been placed. Mission accomplished, it's out of the box, but now there is more to do. Some printers come in a few different pieces for easier shipping, follow directions and assemble it. (Now if you bought an unassembled kit, now you must assemble the entire thing. Good luck.) Some printers might also include shipping bolts to prevent certain pieces from sliding, or tape over end stops to prevent damage. (Most printers are extremely well packed, and have loads of things protecting them so you should look out for things like that.)

Now of course you should have been following the directions supplied by the manufacturer of your printer. Re-read it again and keep looking out for things needed to be done during unboxing/set up. If you miss something, your printer may not work, or could damage itself when turned on. If you believe you have done so, it is time to move onto the next step!

3.2 Calibrating/First Print

Trust me; nothing is more thrilling than your first "test" print. The joy of seeing your printer do its job is amazing! However, you can't just do a test print once it is assembled, there is work to do! You should be following your directions as I have now told you for the umpteenth time, but I will go over what most will basically say.

If you have a 3d printer like most out there, you must go through the hated process of leveling. Leveling your bed is the process of making your printing area (bed) parallel to the nozzle. If you do not do this, it can result in poor bed adhesion and ultimately a failed print.

As long as you print as reasonable sizes, .1-.3mm, you will not need the most perfect leveling, as the printer will in a way compensate for this, as in areas where it is too close, it will end up not being able to extrude a lot of plastic, while in areas where it is too low it will extrude as much as possible, ultimately leveling out to a perfect leveled print. (If this ends up being made into a video series, I will be able to better explain there, so make sure to check if there is one!)

Some printers will not need to have their bed leveled, but if you do and your printer manufacturer doesn't tell you how to, I recommend using a piece of regular printer paper, and starting in the front left corner, moving the back right, back left then from right, making sure there is a tiny bit of resistance as the paper slides under the nozzle. Before you do this, make sure your nozzle was homed in on the Z axis, as it may have been lifted slightly. If you happen to be having issues leveling your bed, check your z axis rods.

Sometimes one side will be lifted or lower slightly more, causing your bed leveling issue. The easiest way to do this is to home all your axis's. Then measure the z axis rod distance from the bottom to where the gantry starts on the side with the end stop.

Now you may as why? Well the side with the end stop is always right, as it will set itself to a set height every time when it hits the end stop. The other z axis rod however, only knows to stop when the end stop on the other side is pressed, so if it had not made it all the way down, it will just stop regardless.

So now, with the measurement from the one z axis rod in mind, measure the other side. Then, manually twist the coupler (What connects the stepper motor to the z axis rod) until it is the same measurement as the other side. Now your axis is level! You may have to check this every once in a while, as one of your z axis stepper motors may be ever so slightly slow, causing it to get out of alignment after so many uses.

Now it is time for your first print! Now many printers will come with the "test file." This is the best option for your first print. Load it up and load your filament as per the directions and start it! Now sit back and enjoy watching your first print come to life. If you start to see plastic peeling from the bed you should probably stop the print as this should not be happening.

Check your bed leveling and temperatures, then try again. However long later when your print is finished, carefully take it off the bed (as you don't want to ruin your first print!) It turned out good hopefully, didn't it? If it didn't happen it is time to check your troubleshooting guide. After this print, usually a small one, it's time to start printing things that you choose!

And we will get to that later on in the guide. Now, more work will be required sadly, as test printers are usually made by the printer gods themselves. They are perfectly tweaked gcode to always work, but if you go straight into printing something else, you will have issues. Follow the rest of the guide to understand how to prepare your printer so you don't get prints with issues!

Chapter 4: Downloading Models

So you have successfully printed your first test model! Or maybe you are still just reading ahead of time, either way we are now at the step of finding your own models to print! This isn't as it seems however, as there are a few things you may run into while doing this that can cause or get you in A LOT of trouble. Don't you worry about it though, ill cover anything you may run into on this path!

4.1 Where Can I get Models From?

Well, there are many places you can download .stl files (the file type used for 3d printers). One of the best known website is Thingiverse, a website owned by MakerBot. Users from all over the world can upload their models to the website and share them. You can find the most simplistic things on Thingiverse such as a hinge to the most complex things like a model of a T-Rex skeleton!

Some people even allow customization of their files through Thingiverse's customization app to be able to change sizes, lettering etc. Another good website is YouMagine, owned by Ultimaker. Their website is similar to Thingiverse with lots of variation in designs and things to print.

Now you may be asking, are there any other websites? Well yes, there are plenty more. I only chose these two for 3 reasons: The websites are reliable and you are not at risk of downloading viruses, most of the models are 3d printable and all the models are free. The 3d printable part I will get to later, and the free part I will hit now.

Many professional designers will make amazing designs, (like a replica of the millennium falcon that opens up to the inside!) And then turn around and sell the files for tons of money. Thingiverse and YouMagine don't allow people to sell the models through their website, so anything on there will always be free! So just search up what you need and pick the best design that fits your needs (or wants)!

Worst scenario is you can't find exactly what you are looking for. This is when you can find a 3D modeler to make it for you. If it something extremely small and easy, you may be able to find someone in a 3d printer group to make one for free, but if your idea is a full scale power armor suit from Fallout 4, you are going to need to find a professional designer, and a few hundred to thousand dollars to pay them! (Okay, you probably won't be designing a full scale suit, as those are expensive to just print, let alone design. If you're idea is say a model of the super bowl trophy, it will probably cost close to $20).

4.2 What Does Ripping From a Game Mean?

Well in simple terms, 3d games use 3d models to be the game. People will "rip" these 3d models from the game and turn them into a .stl file. This may sound really cool, but at the same time is risky. 3D printers have limitations on what they can print; too much details or complicated structures or overhangs will cause the print to fail, even with the most fine-tuned settings. When people design models from scratch, they take into account that a 3d printer must be able to print this, and optimize the file to be printed in ways such as cutting it into smaller pieces, removing unnecessary details, etc.

If you notice the ripped 3d model of a Honda motorcycle, you will see complicated details such as the spokes, engine and more. This design is likely over complicated for your typically printer and will not turn out anywhere close to what you would like to look like. Now I am not saying something like this is not printable, you can try, but don't say I didn't warn you. This kind of print would be more suitable for a more detailed printer such as an SLA printer, but even then it may be iffy.

4.3 Commercial Use

So now you are ready to start selling your printer objects to earn some money. Now some people are good at this, and find something that sells good but there is a problem. You will likely be downloading these models off of a free site such as Thingiverse.

You must pay extremely CLOSE attention to tags such as if it's allowed to be used for commercial use (sell it). In some cases you can just sell it free, others you must give credit, and others you cannot. Even if you bought the design from a website, you must make sure it is allowed to sell them. A great way to avoid all these problems though are to just design your own models, as then you own all the rights to them or have someone else design for you!

Now if neither of these sound appeasing, the final way to avoid legal problems is to just open a 3d shop that prints what is given. (For example 3dhubs does a "Hub" where users upload a .stl file to the website and by formulas you set; it tells them how much it will cost them. This way, you are technically selling the file, even if it can't be used for commercial use. Now this isn't always the most solid way to go about doing it either, some people will dispute this way, but you are unlikely to run into any problems.

Chapter 5: Filament

Okay, most companies give you a maybe a 10 meter test spool of filament. This is usually just enough to print the test print, and if you are following the 3d model downloading portion, you probably are about to start printing something more. This is where you must buy your own filament. Now I will be explaining _MY OPINION_. My filament may work for you but it may not, so I advise for you to read into more reviews of the different brands.

5.1 Filament Types

The most basic filament around would probably be Polylactic Acid (PLA). This is most likely what your sample filament was. The filament usually prints around 200°C to 215°C. It is has good layer adhesion and isn't affected too much by cooling, however it still needs it. It also can be printed without a heated bed. This is also one of the cheaper filament types. A downside though is its lower temperature causes it to warp it in just a hot summer day.

Another common filament is **Acrylonitrile butadiene styrene (ABS)**. This is the same plastic that Lego Bricks are made out of, so it is a very strong plastic. It printers at about 20°C PLA.The downsides though are it requires a heated bed and is very susceptible to warping, as without an enclosure, breezes can make your part cool unevenly causing the layers to warp and not bond correctly. This filament is general not good for beginners are is can be a true challenge. But if you can successfully print it, you have an incredibly strong part.

The 3rd filament I would recommend is **Polyethylene terephthalate (PETG)** [and yes, I know these are hard names, nobody actually uses the full name anyways.] This filament is like the perfect combination I would say. It is quite easy to print like PLA, as it has amazing layer adhesion. It prints at about the same temperatures as ABS, but doesn't require a heated bed or an enclosure to keep the cooling perfect. This filament also is incredibly strong, and has a bit of flex as well. This filament is overall an amazing choice for any project.

Now there are other types of filament such as Ninja Flex, a rubbery very flexible filament, TPU, Nylon, and more but a lot of these filaments are either much more advanced, unneeded, or I don't have enough reliable information to recommend them.

5.2 Filament Brands and Prices

So now I have listed 3 different types of filament, but now is where to buy said filament from. I am more of a budget person, so I do not like to spend $50 for a .5kg roll of plastic. There are many brands out there, but these 3 are the ones I have either heard the best reviews about or have used with great results.

Now we go to Inland filament. This filament, a product of the computer store "Microcenter" is widely thought to be rebranded eSun filament. No matter what it is, I have found that its PLA and PETG turn out amazing prints, as long are you tune your printer settings correctly. (I can't help you there, as spools vary and so do printers) The filament can be ordered from microcenter.com and shipped or picked up directly.

If you live close to a microcenter, I would advise you to buy the filament online and the have it pick up at store. This is because the filament in store is actually a few dollars more expensive then online, so you save some money. The PLA filament costs around $15 a kilogram, while the Petg costs around $18. (I cannot say more for the Abs as I have never used it) All in all, this is one the best cheap filaments.

The next brand is known as Hatchbox. I have used their Pla and it creates amazingly smooth objects. The spools even come in a nice cardboard box that can be used to store your tools and more. This filament can be found on Amazon and a few other retailers, but the problem is the filament is extremely popular. The Pla can usually be found on amazon from $20 to $25 depending on the colors.

The weird colors that nobody buys will always be less than the basics such as white. Overall I have found that Hatchbox also has a better filament diameter compared to inland, which is the reason for these smoother finishes. Now I cannot speak for the Petg, which runs close to $34 on amazon, as the price has always steered me clear of it.

The final brand is Maker Geeks. I have yet to use their filament, but have heard many good reviews about it. They sell filaments such as clear, to even special Pla that is much stronger than the original or even abs. Their filament costs around $18.50, with some of their specialty ranging higher. A good trick to do is if you need bulk, for low costs and don't care about the color is to buy from their "grab bag." For $36 you will get 2 random color rolls of whatever type of filament you choose (with the exception of Raptor PLA, which will add +$15) and occasionally they will even go to $60 for 4 rolls, which saves you $12.

Now your choice of filament is entirely up to you. Ask around people in printer groups what they like or use. Just remember though, just like with 3d printers, the most expensive option is not always the best choice.

Chapter 6: Software

Okay, now you have your printer, models, and plastic. What is next? Well you can't just throw a 3d model into a 3d printer, as it does not understand that format, it much be converted into a file known as gcode for it to print. In these following steps I will show you what to do.

6.1 Slicer Software

The program that converts a 3d model into a gcode file is known as a slicer program. What it does is "slices" the 3d model into layers, with each layer containing information telling the printer simple commands such as, move here, extrude this much, heat to this temperature. So in reality, gcode is not a form of a 3d model, it is just a huge list of commands that form a 3d model.

Now some printers must use special gcode for their printers only, so sometimes you are stuck using one type of slicer software. However most printers are open allowing you to switch freely. Many slicer software offer different things, some even cost money, but when it comes down it, they all do the basic function of converting stl files to gcode.

Now in slicer software, you will have many options to change settings, which is where fine tuning comes in. Temperature, infill, shells, speed and more all is to be adjusted before you export your gcode to your 3d printer. If you need help trouble shooting something, Simplify3D offers an amazing guide, and offers things to change to fix the problems.

6.2 What Slicer Should I Use?

Well, if your printer requires your stock slicer, sorry but you are stuck with it, unless you are good with coding and lots of other goodies. If your printer doesn't need a special slicer, I have 3 different slicer softwares for you to choose from.

The first one is known as Cura. Cura is run by the makers of ultimaker 3d printers. Their software offers many different settings with a simplistic layout. If you only want to see basic settings, you can choose that, or go deeper into and change little tiny things. Many printer companies even offer special "profiles" (settings) for their printer. This program is also free and can be downloaded from ultimaker.com.

The second program is known as Slic3r. (Pretty easy to figure out it's a slicer program right?) Slic3r is an independently run slicer. It offers many advanced options such as cutting objects into smaller pieces, and many more. The only downside I can think of it is it looks older than and not as smooth as many of the new slicer softwares around today. But do not let that fool you; it is still an incredible capable and good slicer.

The final slicer I have on this list is called Simplify3D and by no means is this program simple. Simplify3D I would say has the most options and settings than any other slicer program today. With its ability to add customized supports, switch profiles and settings mid print and more, it by far puts itself near the top of all slicers. There is a catch to this amazing slicer though, one that will set you back $150. Yes, this is one of the few slicers that are not free. This slicer is by no means for beginners, as you would never need such a program when learning. Now, for more professional users, or people that need extreme details and fine tunings, this would fit you quite well.

Now choosing a slicer isn't really that hard, most do the exact same thing. You just have to try them out and see which works better for your needs. Most slicers don't care what printer you are using and printers usually don't care what slicer you use, as long as they both use the same gcode, they can't tell a difference.

6.3 How to Use the Slicer

By now you must have at least chosen a slicer to check out. Using a slicer is fairly simple. For beginners, you will want to stick in the basic section. I cannot go too deep in to how to use the slicer, as they vary from each, but basically you will import your model.

Then you will change the settings for the model, such as the infill, the number of perimeters, etc. Next you will either export the gcode to an SD card and insert that straight into your printer or just print from your computer. Now, I would recommend using an SD card if possible, as if your computer performs an update, crashes, or the wire becomes unplugged, you will lose all your progress on your 3d printer and have to restart.

If your printer for some reason doesn't have an SD card slot, you can always use something like Octoprint, which is a raspberry pi that will plug into your usb slot and act as a mini computer. You can send gcode wirelessly, and not have to worry about your pc shutting off, as the gcode is then saved on the pi. Octoprint also gives you options to view your print while away if you have a camera and even remotely stop your printer! As I said before, printers vary, so read up on your printer on how it accepts gcode files.

Chapter 7: Modding

Now look at it this way. We all strive for perfection. Many prints can get some really amazing prints right off the bat, but of course those printers cost lots of money. If you want to get better prints, you probably will have to tinker with your printer to get them.

7.1 When Should I mod?

Well that is entirely up to you. If you see problems begin to form or see others with the same printers who are getting better results, its problem about time. Some people though choose to mod right off the bat, even if there are no immediate problems present. This future proofs them. It also depends on what you are printing.

Personally, I print items that need fine details and to be smooth, so I don't have to do lots of post printing work. Now if you are just doing lots of prototyping, then you may not care about lines showing. Sometimes printers are also made with design flaws.

For example, my Wanhao printer, the top beam sits too low to be able to get all 180mm of z height, so I modded it to lift it up more. Modding also depends on what kind of printer you have. Most Prusa style printers are very moddable, as their core printer they are based off of uses printed parts to function!

Now the more expensive printers that are built in enclosures, such as the MakerBot, ultimaker and more, are harder to mod, as the way they are designed really doesn't allow for it. Prusa style printers most of the time can be completely disassembled and reassembled to allow for modding, while as more expensive ones, it is much harder to take apart. This doesn't mean you cannot mod more expensive printers; it's just usually harder and sometimes not ever even needed.

7.2 What Should I Mod?

Once again, that is entirely up to you. What you mod is based off of what you can feasibly mod on your printer, and why you should. As the old saying goes, if it's not broke, don't fix it. (Now, it doesn't have to actually be broke, for example, changing a nozzle to a better one is "fixing" a broke nozzle).

Some examples of modding would be z-bracing. Prusa style printers can be unstable near the top, causing z banding, where the layers form deep grooves every so often. A simple solution is to have z braces (rods) attach to the top of the printer, down to the bottom from of the printer. This makes the printer extremely rigid and prevents wobble.

Another example would be fixing bent or crooked z rods. Sometimes in transit the z rods, (what make the printer rise) can get bent. Or when assembled, the rods are nearly impossible to make straight unless it is secured from both sides. If the rod is not attached to the printer at the top, it can wiggle, once again causing z banding.

To fix this, you can install flex couplers instead of solid couplers. A coupler is a small usually plastic of metal piece that attaches the rod to the stepper motor. Flex couplers can bend to compensate for this wiggle, and force it to stop.

Another thing people will mod is their nozzle. Sometimes printer companies use a really crappy nozzle, or bad nozzle set up.

With some extra work, you can switch out the nozzle type, or change from a direct drive set up to a Bowden setup or vis versa.

(A direct drive extruder set up uses a stepper motor right on top of the nozzle heater. This pulls filament to it and pushes it directly into the heater. A Bowden set up, most commonly used on delta style printers will pull filament usually from the bottom the printer or near the top, and push it through a tube that leads to the heater block. Both set ups have their advantages and dis advantages)

What you mod is entirely up to you as I have said before. Usually you can find a community dedicated to your printer, or a similar printer, and they can assist you in how to mod it or what to mod.

When modding though, pay close attention to the amount of money you spend. If you buy a $100 printer but put $500 of mods into it, why didn't you just by a $600 printer that wouldn't need these mods? (Unless of course there was some other reason for doing this).

About the Expert

I am currently a student who makes who works with 3d printing. I have worked with my specific 3d printer, the Wanhao i3 V2 for about a year now and have enjoyed every moment of it. I found 3D printing extremely hard but fascinating from the beginning however I believe anyone who even has the slightest interest should learn more about it and see if they can "connect" with it. I mainly got into 3d printing by seeing people make these incredible things, and I thought to myself, I have to do this. Now, that dream has come true, and I have the ability to work on amazing projects for clients and myself alike, such as BB-8 from Star Wars, the Force Awakens.

HowExpert publishes quick 'how to' guides on all topics from A to Z by everyday experts. Visit HowExpert.com to learn more.

Recommended Resources

- HowExpert.com – Quick 'How To' Guides on All Topics from A to Z by Everyday Experts.
- HowExpert.com/free – Free HowExpert Email Newsletter.
- HowExpert.com/books – HowExpert Books
- HowExpert.com/courses – HowExpert Courses
- HowExpert.com/clothing – HowExpert Clothing
- HowExpert.com/membership – HowExpert Membership Site
- HowExpert.com/affiliates – HowExpert Affiliate Program
- HowExpert.com/writers – Write About Your #1 Passion/Knowledge/Expertise & Become a HowExpert Author.
- HowExpert.com/resources – Additional HowExpert Recommended Resources
- YouTube.com/HowExpert – Subscribe to HowExpert YouTube.
- Instagram.com/HowExpert – Follow HowExpert on Instagram.
- Facebook.com/HowExpert – Follow HowExpert on Facebook.